Who Are the Victims?
A Bipolar Quandary

LIZ JANILL

Bloomington, IN  Milton Keynes, UK

authorHOUSE®

AuthorHouse™
1663 Liberty Drive, Suite 200
Bloomington, IN 47403
www.authorhouse.com
Phone: 1-800-839-8640

AuthorHouse™ UK Ltd.
500 Avebury Boulevard
Central Milton Keynes, MK9 2BE
www.authorhouse.co.uk
Phone: 08001974150

First published by AuthorHouse   4/9/2007

ISBN: 978-1-4259-8657-5 (sc)

Library of Congress Control Number: 2007900235

Printed in the United States of America
Bloomington, Indiana

This book is printed on acid-free paper.

Prologue

Who are the Victims? We are the victims of the disorder called bi-polar; Dorothy, Charles, Liz, Tim, and Ralph. I know you have read and heard a lot of things written about this disorder. Disorder, what an unusual way of describing something that takes on a life of its own and destroys people along the way. It creates conflict, confusion and separation among family members and is something that can never be cured, only partially contained. I am not an educated doctor, but I have talked with, been in the presence of, and consulted with so many psychiatrists and therapists that I feel like I am an expert of this disorder as well. I have a hard time calling bi-polar a "disorder". It is best described as a monster that lies waiting to show its ugly head. That is how Charles, my father, always described it. Consequently, Dorothy's "disorder" was the reason why my recurring childhood nightmare was of my mother turning into a monster and chasing me.

I am not particularly a verbose person, so I don't know how this book will ever really be written. It probably won't be a book, just a novella, or a short story, or a small documentary. I feel like I want to tell this story for several reasons. I don't believe in the therapeutic reason for putting this story in print. It is not for my own therapeutic benefit. It is so that Dorothy's story can be told as well as I, her only daughter can tell it. I will try to be as un-biased as I can be, and since I witnessed all events first person, the only way I know how to tell it is in the first person style.

Another reason I want to tell this story is so that my grandchildren and future generations of my blood line will perhaps have an understanding of what kind of blood they share. They say bi-polar is very hereditary and when my husband and I were getting married, Charles, my father, insisted that we consult a geneticist, which we did. After reviewing my family history, this expert advised us to not have any children, so as not to pass this "bad" gene on. You see, not only did Dorothy have this disorder, but her grandmother had it a long time ago. She died at a time when they did not have adequate drugs or understanding of bi-polar and therefore my great-grandmother died in an insane asylum in Louisiana. She had been locked up for her own safety, where she died not knowing who she was or any of her family.

I have seen a lot of books written by the diagnosed bipolar person; how they feel and what their delusional thoughts are. Therefore, this book is about the other victims, the family and friends, who every day help maintain and care for those who are diagnosed bipolar.

This is especially true for the children of a bipolar mother, and what we felt and witnessed.

This story will be told in the best chronological order that can be remembered. And please remember, as bizarre as some of the scenarios sound, they are very real in the world of severe mental illness.

Dorothy as Homecoming Queen at 17 years of age.

Chapter 1

Dorothy Jo Brigham was born in Shreveport, Louisiana, February 24, 1931. She is my mother. Her father was a man who worked for the railroad and her mother was a gregarious, German woman who loved to laugh and drink beer. Granny B., as we called her, was married three times and my mother had several step brothers and sisters. None of this, in my opinion, had anything to do with her bipolar disorder.

People in today's time would say that children are being affected by their parent's divorces. Dorothy may have been, but the bi-polar "monster" was such a huge thing, that the idea of a simple divorce causing this behavior in Dorothy is simply absurd. I always say that everyone has a story to tell about their life and this is just ours.

Dorothy was a beauty. I am not just saying this because she was my mother. She won beauty contests. When she was a senior in high school, she was voted homecoming queen. In case you don't know, back then in small towns, the football homecoming was a complete town event. The Main Street of Bossier City was closed down, just for the parade that would include the high school bands, football players and, of course, the queen and her "court".

All of these groups would be presented on floats that would drive down Main Street in a huge parade. Their pictures would appear in the paper and the whole town would arrive to see and be seen. You should understand that only the most popular and beautiful people were ever elected to those honors. I want you to see this side of Dorothy, because she was once a very popular, beautiful and well liked person among her peers. Charles remembers his wife in their early years of marriage as being a hard worker and full of life. She was a contributing partner in their marriage and was very creative. This was to change in a few, very short years.

At the age of twenty six, and after having given birth to three children, Dorothy started exhibiting what appeared to be depression. She was very belligerent and defiant and cried a lot. Charles took her to the doctor and the first diagnosis was post-partum depression and exhaustion. So after spending some time in the hospital a specialist was brought in to consult with her.

After observing her for a week he called Charles in for a conference. This psychiatrist said that Dorothy was not suffering from post-partum depression, but something much more serious. He diagnosed her as bi-polar with delusions and paranoia. He explained that this was caused by a chemical imbalance and that there was no cure for this condition. Back then, the medical world did not have excellent medications to moderate this disorder, this "monster".

The doctor's medical opinion was to place her into an asylum because this disorder is very hereditary. He told Charles that the children had already inherited the gene; they didn't need the influence of their mother in their formative years. The doctor told Charles that he had the right to place her into an asylum, because at that time the husband or spouse had the right to do this, or he could do what he could to keep her medicated and living as normal a life as possible. Charles was sent home for a week to think about this and then to make a decision. What you need to know about Charles is that he was orphaned when he was six years old. His mother died of an un-known illness and his father contracted tuberculosis and was sent to a sanitarium in Arkansas where he eventually died. This set of circumstances sent Charles on a necessary journey spent with whatever relative had the money at the time to take on another child to feed and raise.

After the conference, Charles went home and looked at his three children from the ages of five, three, and eighteen months old. He decided that they should have a mother in their lives no matter what. He was not going to be the one to take our mother from us. Later that week he went back to the doctor and said, do what you can for my wife. He was going to take her home to her children and not place her into an insane asylum. Obviously, these facts came from Charles because I was the eighteen month old and not aware of what was going on in my life or what the future with my mother and the bipolar monster would entail.

Chapter 2

   The first incident with Dorothy that I remember was when I was five years old. Charles had a dairy farm and milked over one hundred cows twice a day. The life of this kind of farmer starts at 300AM with the first milking of those cows which lasts until around 700AM. The second milking of each day begins around 400PM and lasts until sundown. This was Charles's life every single day, with no day off, not even on the weekends. One early morning, after Charles left the house at 300AM, Dorothy woke us up, the three children, who were myself and my two older brothers, Tim and Ralph, and she told us we were going for a ride at 300AM. She told us not to bother getting dressed as she was not getting dressed either. She did have the presence of mind to write Charles a note that I remember vividly. She got a pencil and wrote on the surface of the kitchen table. It was one of those old farm tables that had a white enamel finish on the top. She wrote that she had taken us for a ride in the country and would be back later. It wasn't the fact that she had gotten us up in the middle of the night that puzzled me, but the fact that, why didn't she just get a piece of paper to write him a note on, instead of writing the note right on the tabletop itself?

The four of us just rode around in the car with our pajamas and nightgowns on and watched the sunrise in the early morning. She stopped at a roadside fruit stand and bought us some fruit for breakfast and then we drove home.

By this time Charles had seen that his family was gone and had called the police and had everyone in town looking for us.

We drove up to the house and the police were there and Charles was in a panic. Dorothy calmly said that we had just been for a ride and hadn't he seen the note she left? From that time forward I noticed that she started to become more delusional and belligerent and was soon taken to the hospital. The monster had started to raise its ugly head and became an unwelcome member of the family.

Each time Dorothy had a hospital stay she was admitted to the psychiatric ward where she would stay for an average of three months. Charles always wanted her to have the best possible care. She always stayed in the private hospital even though; with her diagnosis she was un-insurable.

Charles would always be responsible for a hospital bill that would always be thousands of dollars. He would work out a payment plan and just manage to pay off one three month stay when she would be re-admitted for another one. This started a life for us kids of just living from one psychotic episode of our mother to the next one. When she was at home we were told to be quiet in the house and not to "rock her boat" in any way.

The farm house we lived in for twenty years was very unique in a weird way. It really was only half a house, as only one half was ever completed. It consisted of one large room used for watching TV and a table for eating every meal. It had a very small, galley type kitchen, one small bedroom and one small bathroom.

The bathroom had a toilet, a hot water heater that stood next to the toilet, and a shower. There was only one sink in the whole house and that was in the kitchen. We cooked, cleaned dishes, brushed our teeth, and shaved, all of us every day, out of the same sink in that small kitchen. In addition to those rooms, it had a small double garage. It was this garage that was converted into bedrooms for my brothers and me. A wall was constructed down the middle of the garage to create two bedrooms, one for me and the other for my brothers to share. But the roll-up garage doors stayed and were the outside walls of our rooms. My father built a huge screen frame that totally covered the outside of my garage door, so that in the summer, I could raise the door and have a whole bedroom wall of screened in outside world. The house had no central air-conditioning so this worked as well as it could. It was like camping out every night in the summer. In the winter, I would bring the garage door back down, where it would stay closed until the spring. Obviously, there was no insulation, so I froze in the winter and burned up in the summer. I told everyone that I lived in the garage, and it was literally true.

Therefore, in this small farmhouse setting, we children were sternly warned to help our mother to live as calm and peaceful existence as she could each day. I don't remember wanting for anything materialistic growing up. I knew we were not rich, and everything we had, both monetarily and emotionally went to the maintenance and care of Dorothy. If we were playing and wanted to be loud children, we always had to go outside.

The household was always focused on staying quiet and with as little chaos as possible. The daily life did not revolve around the children. The daily life revolved around what Dorothy needed and keeping her calm and the "monster" at bay.

After her diagnosis, parts of the doctor's orders were for her to get a nap every afternoon, which she did every day. She would put on her nightgown after lunch and go to bed. Our dairy farm had an active railroad that ran the length of the front property. On one occasion, Dorothy got out of her bed during her nap, with her nightgown on, and got into the car and started to follow the train as far north as she could go. She went as far as Arkansas this time. The police were called and they found her. Her explanation was that God had told her to follow the train.

To give Dorothy some credit, in her "good" time she could function at a near normal level, although highly medicated on anti-psychotic drugs. She was a great cook and always made sure we went to church every Sunday. Not a great house keeper, which I found out early in life, would be my main job anyway. Her next episode that I remember was when I was eleven years old. She was not sleeping at all at night and would just wander the house.

I have memories of her standing in the dark doorway of my room at night. Sometimes she would come in very excited, in the middle of the night to tell me something that just could not wait until the morning, or she would just stand in the doorway in the dark and be either laughing or crying hysterically.

I would lie in my bed and hold my breath and try to make her believe that I was sleeping and hope that she would go away soon. This went on a lot and I did not get good quality sleep. I was always tired and suffered from fever blisters on my lips for worry and lack of sleep when I was eleven years old.

Then one day in the summer, Charles and my brothers were working in the hayfield as they did every summer. So I am at home alone with Dorothy. She had been angry, not sleeping well and had been talking nonsense for a few days. These were always the tell-tale signs that she was "getting sick" again. No matter how many anti-psychotic drugs she took every day, there always came a time when her tolerance level would be so high, that no matter how many drugs she took, the "disorder" would always be stronger that the drugs. It was very hot and she closed every window and door in the house. Remember we had no air conditioning.

She made me sit in the hot living room with her and she closed the door. She said that Jesus was coming that day and he had chosen her and me to be there to help him with his great return to earth.

She got all dressed up in her very best Sunday outfit, makeup on, dress shoes and sat in the rocking chair and sobbed and laughed hysterically all morning. She was so excited that God had chosen her and me to make his great return to earth. I was scared to death. Having been raised in the Baptist church, I halfway wanted to believe her.

I had been taught that Jesus was returning to gather the faithful and I was still young enough to want to believe what my mother was saying was true. But on the other hand I knew she was sick and was delusional. I was so scared that I just had to leave the house for a while. I remember getting on my bicycle and taking a ride around the neighborhood where I had several friends.

I passed each house and wanted to go in and ask their parents to come help me with my mother, but how do you begin to ask for help with some one who is delusional and waiting for God to return?

I went back home because I was afraid she would hurt herself. She then took me into one of the bedrooms and told me to sit on the floor with my legs out in front of me and to close my eyes. She then got one of my brother's balls, a superball it was called, and she threw it at me. It bounced off my head and rolled onto the floor and she said I could get up, but not to look around at all and leave the bedroom.

Then a friend of my brothers knocked at the front door and I was so excited that someone was there to help me with her. But she walked outside to talk to him, so he would not see that we were sitting in a hot and steamy house with the windows closed in the middle of summer and proceeded to have a normal conversation with him.

She immediately walked back in and started to talk about God still coming and what a wonderful day it was for us. It is shocking how the mentally ill can sometimes go from delusional to what seems like normal instantly. I just stared at her in amazement.

Finally that evening Charles and my brothers returned from their day in the hayfield. I met Charles at the back gate, reached up and grabbed him by the shirt collar and said. "Get her out of our house or

I will kill her myself!" He got a grimace on his face and said he knew she was not well and that he had just waited too long to get her to the hospital.

The "monster" had reared its ugly head again. Another joyous job we always had was trying to convince her to go to the hospital. The mentally ill are convinced that what they are thinking is absolutely correct and the last thing they want to do is be admitted to a double lock down padded area in a psychiatric ward of a hospital.

So Charles would call Dorothy's sister, and the preacher and they would eventually convince her that she was not thinking clearly and just needed to have her medications adjusted by the doctor.

Chapter 3

Every time we took her to the hospital it was with an entourage. Charles, Dorothy, the three kids, Dorothy's sister and the preacher. All the way on the drive to the hospital Dorothy would be laughing hysterically that God had a plan for us all and that this was wonderful. We always made sure she sat in the middle, not near a door; because we were afraid she would jerk the door open and throw herself out. Seven people would show up at the emergency room and meet the doctor to take her for her next three month stay. This happened every single time, year after year.

Parts of Dorothy's delusions were that the family was torturing her and abusing her. Especially Charles, so she would not believe anything we said to her when she was delusional. This is one of the most frustrating things about this disorder. We are the ones who love her the most and spend each minute of each day just thinking of her needs.

But we are the ones she hates the most and does not trust the most and thinks we are mis-treating and abusing her. Believe me, there were many times that I wanted to be mean to her, but she was just so pitiful and sick that there was no point in ever hurting her in any way.

This hospital stay, when I was eleven years old, was a turning point in my life. I was told to stay in the waiting room of the psychiatric ward while my father and the doctor helped her get settled, but I followed them in.

I saw her get undressed and put on nothing but a hospital gown, then they locked her into a stark bare room that looked like a prison. It only had a single metal bare bed, one night stand with nothing on it and a window that was covered with a metal mesh.

She looked wild and much disheveled as she always looked in her delusional state. She had large dark circles under her eyes because she had not slept in about two weeks and she was crying and begging us to take her back home.

This was the first time I had seen this and would not certainly be the last time either, but at the age of eleven, I swore to myself that from then on two things were going to happen in my life. One was that I would never be alone in the house with her ever again and two, I made sure that I would never be like her.

This was my role model and the person that I was supposed to imprint myself upon since I was her only daughter. From then on, if I found myself doing something that I thought she would do, I changed immediately. I made sure at the age of eleven that I was not going to turn out that way and would not emulate her ever.

After this I never allowed myself to be really close to her emotionally because I never knew when the "monster" would return and cause me emotional trauma.

It was easier to hold her at an arm's length and not think of her in the traditional mother role, but just as someone I needed to care for and to protect. Somehow, we the children took responsibility for her even when we were young. The mothering aspect of our lives was pretty much history at this point.

This is the age for me that I became really aware that my mother was severely ill and I wanted to understand what it was more fully. This time when she was in the hospital, I would get up late at night and find Charles alone in the living room.

He would be in the rocking chair, by an open screen door. It was summer, hot, no air-conditioning and I could see the glow of his cigarette in the dark. I would ask him questions about this illness and in the dark he would tell me the details. I, at the age of eleven, really did not know how to process it all, but being a girl, I wanted to talk things to death. But after this we never discussed how sick our mother was among us. After each hospital stay and manic episode she had, I wanted so badly to just shake her and say "Do you know what you did to us, do you remember all those crazy things you said and did?" I wanted to confront her and tell her how much she scared me or hurt me.

But when she would come home from having had shock-treatments, it would be so obvious how very fragile she still was emotionally, that it would harm her more to discuss things.

She never remembered any of the craziness she had thought or done after her treatments, so it would do more harm than good to confront her with her actions.

We would bring her home and continue with life and never discuss anything. We just continued to live in apprehension and fear of the next time the monster appeared.

But as the daughter of a bipolar mother and knowing I have inherited her genes, I always lived with the fear of turning out like her. I was afraid of transforming into someone who was delusional and paranoid for most of my childhood. Not until I was about twenty five years old was I able to relax and realize that I was normal. I had always felt like maybe this condition could possibly be passed on to me.

The small town we lived in was very good to us when they knew Dorothy was "having one of her spells". We never elaborated just how sick she was; most people just probably thought she suffered from depression. I would have given anything if all we had to contend with was depression. The church people would always bring us food, especially on Sunday. One of the family friends came and got me. She packed up all my things and I stayed with her and her family for one three month episode. She was a wonderful role model for me and I attribute most of my mothering skills I have to her.

I am sure she just thought that it was not appropriate for me to stay at home with just my brothers and father for those three months. Charles was grateful for any help he could get. Her family was 3 sons and a husband and it was obvious she was Queen of the house. She considered me the daughter that she never had. This mother figure was strong and confident and I loved her a lot. I also feel like Charles orchestrated my going with other strong women for some quality normal time with them.

Another family friend would also pack me up and keep me for two or three weeks.

She was another of the female role models that I formed myself around. I learned how to be sophisticated from her. Her back yard was a beautiful assortment of blooming flowers and water fountains. I learned how to be a regal woman, how to love gourmet food and the better things in life. Her English was always spoken perfectly, and she insisted that mine was the same. She would correct my country way of talking. She would take me to the most elaborate flower shows in Shreveport where I had never seen anything so beautiful in my life. After I had been a grown woman for many years, I went to her house to visit. It had been probably twenty five years since I had been in her house and the minute I stepped into the door I just started to surprisingly cry. The memory of her soft, plush carpet that I loved to walk on barefoot, the smells of Lysol, the feel of fresh air conditioned air, and the beauty of richly colored tiffany lamps, bombarded me immediately. The most wonderful memories of my childhood just rushed over me and caught me by surprise.

I had forgotten what a refreshing respite her house had been for me.

I would go with the rest of my family to visit Dorothy every Sunday afternoon when she was well enough for visitors. Charles would point out to me the red marks that were on each side of her temples. That was where she was receiving shock treatments. These were very barbaric and severely traumatic.

But for Dorothy this was the only way, back then, for her to get her thinking back to normal. Tim remembers the first time she received shock treatments. He was seven years old and I was only eighteen months. She did not remember us as her children when she came home from the hospital. It took several weeks and the family to convince her that we were indeed her children. Our own mother had forgotten who we were due to this disorder and because of the severe shock treatments which were the only treatment that would work for her at the time.

Chapter 4

No amount of medicine that was available then would be strong enough to bring her back home to us. That is why the shock treatments were used. After she came home from the hospital when I was eleven years old, I took over the role of taking care of a lot of the house. I had cooked at home while she was gone and done the laundry. It was a miracle because at age eleven, I really did not know what I was doing. I just knew I had to do my part to keep the family going every day. This time she was especially mad at Charles for supposedly abusing her and she had flushed her wedding rings down the toilet. We only found this out after we had searched for her rings all over the house. Charles then asked the psychiatrist to ask her about it and she admitted to the flushing. They were a beautiful three band set with several rows of diamonds. I am sure Charles spent much of his savings on those rings when they had gotten married.

So after she got well and came home, I went with her to pick out a new wedding band. This one was a very plain silver band, very different from her original one. I remember standing at the jewelry counter with the man working there helping her pick one out and he asked, after looking at me, the eleven year old, what had happened to her first wedding set. How do you tell the salesperson that in your delusional state of confusion that you flushed your wedding bands down the toilet? So she just politely said that they were lost.

After this episode Dorothy went for several years doing pretty well. My brothers went to college and I was left home with her. This is when the third female role model became important to me. I was jealous of my brothers for being able to leave the house, so I basically moved in at the age of fifteen with my best friend and her single mother. This faux mother was there for me in my teenage years to help me with questions about teenage female issues, like sex, drugs, and the opposite sex. She loved to cook and it seemed like she always knew when we would be home. On the stove we would find meals like mashed potatoes, chicken fried steak, and vegetables ready to eat every time. She loved to drink Cokes and had plenty of those as well. She was not a conventional mother and thought outside the box. She was open-minded and fun loving. This appealed to my liberal, rebellious side that I really felt more natural and comfortable with. To her I owe a huge "Thank you" for being there when I needed guidance.

Sometimes I would be at home during the school week. I remember leaving for school at 730AM and Dorothy would be sitting in the rocking chair in her nightgown, just rocking. Later when I would come home from school, at 400PM, she would be in exactly the same spot, same attire, still rocking. From the rocking chair she would start barking orders for me to sweep and mop the floors, start the laundry and start cooking dinner.

Needless to say, I became angry. I had been at school working and studying all day and it was obvious that she had done nothing all day but a lot of rocking. She was very good at believing she was a queen and loved to order people around. I finally realized that this was one of the few times I had seen her in the depression mode of manic-depression, because I believe most of her time was spent in the manic phase.

As time passed, my brothers each got married and I went to x-ray school. While in x-ray school a second thing happened that we as children or our parents did not need in life. Charles had an industrial accident that blinded him for life. He had sold out of the dairy business and was working as an inspector for the State of Louisiana. He had a tank of anhydrous ammonia blow up on him and it almost killed him.

Chapter 5

Dorothy was actually working as a sitter for old people in nursing homes. She was at work and got the call that Charles was in the emergency room and was severely hurt   She was immediately overwhelmed and hysterical as she called me to come get her and go to the hospital with her. I did all the paper work and talked to the doctor and Charles stayed in the ICU for two weeks before he came home. Initially, we were just glad he was alive, but we soon found out that his eyes were so severely burned that he would never see again. I was nineteen years old then and Charles and Dorothy were forty five years old. My brothers and I were in shock. Not only did we have a severely mentally ill mother, but now we had a handicapped blind father to care for.

During this time I met my husband Gerard. Looking back on this, I dated some men, but sub-consciously, I wanted someone who was concrete, a man with integrity and a man with no chaos or wild ideas. I needed safety and security at home above all else and would not settle for anything else and that is exactly what I got. We had two sons and I decided to be the best mother I could possible be, contrary to what I personally had. I wanted them to know that I would be there for them, no matter what, that I could be the one they could call when they were in trouble, or needed help, because I never had that from my mother growing up.

I never had any one to call for help or a mother to talk to late at night. I also never told my sons about their grandmother. I wanted them to know her in the good times, and to love her as they should love a grandmother. I did not want them to know about this "disorder" that could possibly be passed on to them until they were older and mature enough to understand it.

I was the queen of the house of men, a lover of the finer things in life, and able to live outside of the box, just as I had learned from my 3 substitute mothers. Every night of my young sons' lives, I would tuck them in, kiss them goodnight, and tell them," I love you". I made sure their closet doors were closed, as I always made sure mine was closed as well. The memory of Dorothy and the "monster" standing in my dark bedroom doorway never stopped haunting me.

Charles now needed extreme care and went to Houston for about thirty surgeries over a three years period to try to salvage his eyesight. I think during this time, Dorothy held herself together with a lot of medicine, because she knew that Charles needed more care than she did at the moment. On the occasion of one of Charles's surgeries, I went to be with him in Houston because Dorothy was not in the frame of mind to go with him. I was in my mid-twenty's and had just found out that I was two months pregnant with my first son.

The doctor came in just before the surgery to explain that he was going to take Charles's eye out so he could access the optic nerve and try to repair the damage behind his eye. He also told us that Charles would not be under general anesthesia but would be given a local injection around his eye for the entire surgery. It was un-believably frightening to hear. When the doctor left the room Charles came over to give me a hug and he started crying on my shoulder. This was my rock and the man who had kept the family together all these years and he was scared and crying.

He then proceeded to tell me how much he needed a shoulder to cry on and someone to lean on in his time of fear and tribulation. He said that he could not lean on Dorothy for his own support because of her illness. I realized then that their marriage had also been victimized by this "disorder", this "monster". Dorothy was an emotional shipwreck on the shore laid out on the sand in a million different pieces. How could her husband ever hope to get any support from her?

Charles never left Dorothy physically or monetarily, but he did leave her emotionally for his own survival. After this episode Charles would find different female friends who would listen to his fears, and be companions to him emotionally where his wife, Dorothy could not provide this for him. As an adult I could understand this, but as the daughter of Dorothy, it was very hard for me to accept. But I did know that if you are not getting the things for your own personal survival from your spouse that you will find it somewhere else. That is what Charles had to do. Much to the extreme disappointment of all of us, Charles never gained his eyesight back.

Dorothy had only one episode of being manic during this time. I remember that we had a family meeting with the doctor. Charles had asked us, the kids, since we were now adults, to help him with Dorothy.

It was too big a job for him anymore, working with the doctors and the insurance company and the various other people it took to keep Dorothy in the real world. We were at a family meeting one of the times Dorothy was in the psychiatric-ward in the hospital.

The doctor told us that she was still not well and probably would not return home for a few more weeks.

We asked him if we could see her and he recommended that we not visit with her at that time, but he could not stop us from seeing her if that was what we wanted. Charles and Tim left the conference room and went toward the elevator, but Ralph and I decided we would visit her in her room. When we entered her room we found her naked under the bed in a fetal position. There are no words to describe how we felt seeing our mother in this position. We were just in a state of shock and disbelief. This was an extreme example of depression that had basically paralyzed her. Normal people get depressed and we cry, or go to bed. We are just sad for an afternoon or a few days. This is another difference between manic-depression and the normal world.

Their emotions swing as far to both sides of euphoria and depression as a human can possible go. A lot of the time bipolar people commit suicide because their depression is too painful to live with. We at least were fortunate that she never committed suicide or talked about it that I know of. After that, if the doctor said he would not recommend going to see Dorothy, believe me we did not go.

Another episode occurred with Dorothy being delusional and Charles called me to say that she was not doing well and he was scared. One night when they had just gone to bed, Dorothy sat straight up in bed and looked at Charles and said "They told me to kill you". She was talking about the people who were talking to her inside of her head. So he stayed up all night and called me in Texas early in the morning to say "I need you". I got on the first plane I could get and went to help him.

All that day Dorothy was delusional, crying and laughing at the same time. She said that someone named Jay was coming from God and was holding a meeting with all of us. He was coming to heal everyone who was sick and that he, Jay, had promised her that she could be the first one healed. She was so excited and just sobbed and sobbed about how she was going to be healed. What I remember most is how sad it was that even in her delusional state, she knew she was sick and it meant a lot to her to be the first one to be healed. We had been on the phone with her doctor all day and we were taking her to the hospital the next morning. So that night we were trying to just keep her calm by watching some television. I was lying on the floor and she was sitting on the couch, just laughing and crying and talking to the people in her head.

I finally got so tired of it, I told her to just quit talking to them because we were tired of hearing it. She got up off the couch at 1000PM and got dressed in her Sunday best clothes, hose and dress shoes. She applied all her makeup and was looking her best because "Jay" was coming and she had to be ready to be healed first.

She walked the hallway of the house all night long, in her heels and crying and laughing. I pushed the bed against the wall of the bedroom I was sleeping in and turned my back to the wall, so I would know that at least the back side of me was safe. I stayed awake all night listening to her walk the hallway sobbing and laughing. My childhood "monster" was alive and quite active.

The next day, Charles and I, along with the preacher and Dorothy's sister, admitted Dorothy to the hospital where her doctor placed her once again in the psychiatric-ward to begin the process of getting her mind right. I went home and just cried. It is so sad to see your mother so excited, upset and delusional. It was something that I never got used to. Taking her to be admitted to the hospital always upset all of us to the extreme. She stayed for a few months and returned to Charles like she always did.

Chapter 6

Charles decided that they should build a new home with a divided living area with the idea of hiring a live in care giver for the two of them. After the new home was built, Charles and Dorothy moved in and hired a lady, Linda to live with them to provide care for both of them. Linda would drive them to their doctor's appointments, go to the store, cook and clean.

This seemed to be working well and everyone was at ease knowing that they were being cared for. Until, once again Dorothy's medicine started to not work and she became very agitated and aggressive toward Linda. She accused her of having an affair with Charles and just generally started to not trust her. She wanted her out of the house.

One night Dorothy wanted Linda to take her to Bossier City for a hamburger. Linda had just returned from having a weekend off while another lady had helped to care for Charles and Dorothy. Since Linda had just walked in the door, she told Dorothy that she did not want to drive back to Bossier right then. This made Dorothy very angry and she tried to stab the Linda with a fork. Dorothy then got the car keys and chased Linda around the house trying to stab her with the car keys.

Charles in the meantime had been at the neighbor's house. Her name was Mary and she and Charles came into the house about the time Dorothy was angry at Linda. Charles and Mary were able to calm Dorothy.

Later, in the same night, Dorothy was very angry at Charles for allegedly abusing her and somehow locked him outside the house after 1000PM. She had everyone locked out, but Charles finally convinced her to let Linda in and he spent the night with Mary at the house next door.

That night Linda did spend the night with Dorothy. She had her door locked and the next day she resigned and moved out. Charles convinced Dorothy along with her doctor at the time to take herself to the hospital to have her medicine re-evaluated.

Chapter 7

At this time I had a sister in law who did not get along with Charles. They just were two people who could not see eye to eye on anything. She would frequently be very rude to my parents, but because she was my sister in law, I never would say anything to her. I would tell my parents not to let her talk rude to them. They were afraid if they voiced their opinions, that they would lose contact with their son, my brother Ralph. This went on for years and I don't want to grace the sister in law with the details of her rude and abusive behavior toward them.

I have to include her here because she was integral to what happens next in Dorothy's life. Dorothy never really had any lady friends except for her sister. She had church acquaintances but no close friends. I understand this is common with bipolar people.

Most normal people don't want to spend quality time with bipolar people after they realize that they are as ill as they are. I think this is sad, because they have a lot to offer, but it is hard to get around the illness to see the real person inside. If you have a choice, most people are friends from a distance, and won't develop an intimate friendship with them.

The reason I include this is that Dorothy thought her daughter in law was a close friend and would confide things to Ruth. When Charles was first blinded he received a money settlement from the company where his accident occurred. It was really not much money considering that he lost his eyesight at the age of forty five. He lost his means of making a living, and had a severely mentally ill spouse to support. We, the children were very protective of what money he did have. Some how this sister in law wanted his money and proceeded to convince Dorothy to divorce Charles. We were sure that Dorothy would lose her half of whatever money she would get in a divorce and be poverty bound in her later years of life. Remember that she had no insurance and would spend several thousands of dollars each hospital stay. So this situation was a real concern to us.

During this particular hospital stay, Ruth would visit Dorothy in the psychiatric-ward and tell her that she did not have to do what the doctor said. If she did not want to take her medicine, she did not have to and to just live her life as she wanted to. Well, that is basically true, but was going against everything the doctor was trying to accomplish with Dorothy. If Dorothy did not take anti-psychotic drugs she would go into a permanent manic state of mind and not be able to function in the real world.

The only visual I can give of her manic state is when you go to the zoo and see a wild tiger behind bars and he just paces back and forth with a wild look in his eye, and never relaxes. This is how I have seen Dorothy.

Add to that, delusional thoughts of the government spying on her and living in a complete state of fear. Because Dorothy really believed everything Ruth told her, and because, I believe, she so wanted to have a real friend, Dorothy refused to co-operate with the medical staff and take her medicine. That was her right, to not take her medicine. In America, you can't be forced to take medicine. You can be as crazy as you want to be. You can verbally threaten to harm yourself and other people. Nothing can be done to stop you until you actually do harm to yourself or to someone else. The medical staff called the family in for a meeting to discuss what to now do with Dorothy. Present at the meeting were the doctor, his assistant, the nurses, Charles, Tim, Ruth, and I. Ruth came because my brother Ralph was out of the country and she felt compelled to represent him there.

The nurses brought Dorothy in, as well, in her non-medicated state. She had on a hospital gown and someone had given her a tube of bright red lipstick. She not only had the lipstick all over and around her lips, it was also all over her cheeks and forehead. She sat down in the circle where we all were and just started to laugh hysterically and cry at the same time. She was holding her belly and just roaring a wild laugh. Tim and I looked at each other and said" Who the hell gave her that lipstick?" because we knew to keep those things away from her.

With this going on, the doctor began to tell us that Dorothy had decided to be in non-compliance with the medical staff and not take her medicine. Further more, she had dismissed her doctor because she was convinced he was trying to kill her and she did not trust him anymore. The doctor had been her physician for a long time and he said that he thought he could not help her anymore because he had lost her trust. Trust in mentally ill patients is a major factor for their successful treatment. If they become convinced that you are not someone they can trust, then you cannot get them to co-operate. Because of the things that my sister in law had been telling Dorothy, we had lost the doctor that helped us everyday with this disorder. The doctor looked at Charles, Tim and I and said that Dorothy was operating in what he called a "hypo-manic" state and that he had to dismiss her from the hospital. We were told to come get her in two days and take her home like that.

We had never taken her home from the hospital in the same mental state as she went in. She always would comply and take her medicine, which would get her thinking straight and come home in what we knew as her normal mode. So Tim and I knew we had to take her home to live with our blind father in a hypo-manic state of mind. We were in shock!

Dorothy stood up, with the bright red lipstick all over her face, and went to the middle of this circle of her family and medical staff and began to dance around in a circle, laughing and saying "I'm a little devil, I'm a little devil" and having a wonderful time. Tim and I referred to this later as "Mothers Little Devil Dance". The medical staff then took her out of the room and the doctor asked Ruth to leave. This is when he told us that the staff had witnessed Ruth telling Dorothy to not do what he, the doctor wanted and that she did not have to take the medicine if she did not want to. The doctor wanted to know if there was something we could do about our sister in law. I became instantly infuriated and asked the medical staff to record what they had seen and heard in Dorothy's chart. I knew that her medical chart was a legal document. I then went home and called my brother, Ralph, who at the time was working on an international oil rig in New Guinea, on the other side of the world. I called him on a satellite phone and told him to keep his wife away from our mother because she was being detrimental to our mother's health. I also obtained a restraining order against her ever being in the presence of Dorothy. It takes a sick mind to mess around with a person who has a diagnosed sick mind as it is. I had previously convinced Dorothy to sign over to me her medical and business power of attorney and I intended to use what power I had to protect Dorothy from anyone who would do her harm, even if it was a family member.

When Ruth found out about these things, she changed her phone to block our telephone numbers from calling her house. She called me to say that I was not to ever contact my brother again, even if someone died. I was not to call their house ever again. We had lost our brother and I feared that this would happen. But when it came to protecting Dorothy, I was willing to do what I had to do, even at the cost of losing my brother. Tim and I told Ralph that we loved him and he was welcome to return to the family when he got rid of his wife. She had been detrimental to our sick mother and she was not going to be tolerated any more. We then went twelve years without having any contact with Ralph. It was his choice, as he told us that he would have to support his wife's decision and stand by her. Another example of being victimized was losing our brother for twelve years to a scenario caused by this disorder.

All of these events were more than Charles could emotionally handle. He told Tim and I that Dorothy was now our responsibility. Charles would try to help with decisions, but Tim and I would have to make final decisions with the medical staff and take care of her medical bills. We the children were to be her total guardians. We were accepting of this because we would never leave her no matter what happened. We would be there for her and care for her.

We consulted with the medical staff for the next two days to plan what do to next. One of the nurses recommended that we take Dorothy to court to have her in-voluntarily committed to an asylum because she was in non compliance with her doctors.

This thought was something we did not think we could ever do. I remember telling that nurse that we would never be able to live with taking her to court and that it would kill our father to do this to her. So they recommended that we take her to a nursing home that specialized in mentally ill patients and see if they could work with her to take her medicines. When I talked to Dorothy about it, of course in her hypo-manic state of euphoria, there was no way she was going there of her own free will. So I used my power of attorney and registered her there anyway. I could not take her home to live, so this was our best choice at the time. I checked her out of the hospital still laughing and crying at the same time and took her to this place. I told her we were just going to look at it. When I got her there, the nurses got her involved with a game that the other patients were playing and I left.

I went to Charles' house and cried. I could not believe I had tricked her into staying there, but she had left us no choice. Tim and I had already placed her things in a room, so she had her personal items and a bed and TV and all the other comforts that we knew she needed. Later that night I called her to tell her that as long as she was in non-compliance with her medicine that she would have to stay there and she called me a bitch and hung up.

We had explained our situation to the medical staff at this nursing home and they were so wonderful with trying to help us get Dorothy back to her normal way of thinking. They would put the prescribed anti-psychotic drugs into her carton of milk and try to get her to drink it.

But she was so not trusting of anyone, such that if she saw that her milk was open in any way, she would pour it out. She was very agitated, not on any medicine and not sleeping at night. I would visit her periodically and take her shopping. Once we were in a shopping mall and she wanted me to buy her a new dress, so we found her one in a dress shop. She was wearing slacks and a button down shirt and went into the dressing room to try on the dress. When she came out she had put the dress on over her slacks and shirt and said she liked it and for me to buy it.

We got to the counter to pay for the dress and the clerk said, "Don't you want me to put that dress into a bag for you?", and Dorothy very angrily said, "No, I am wearing it out just like this".

The clerk looked at me and I said, "It's OK, let her wear it how she wants". I paid for the dress and we left the shop and walked through the mall with Dorothy wearing slacks, and button down shirt and over that a beautiful new dress. We got a lot of funny looks in that mall as we finished our shopping.

During her stay in this nursing home, Dorothy convinced the staff to let her go for walks on the street outside the front door. They would watch her as she walked and got some fresh air, except for one time she was walking and did not come back. They called me to say that they had lost her and were calling the police. Before the police could arrive, I got a call from Dorothy myself. She was laughing and said "Guess where I am?" I was afraid to ask her, so she told me she was at home. We had left their house empty and Charles was staying with the next door neighbor, Mary.

He was paying her to care for him and this was working for all of us really well. I asked Dorothy how she got there and how did she get into the house. She laughed and said that my wonderful sister in law had picked her up and took her home.

Dorothy then used a rock and broke a window in the back of the house and crawled in through it. I tried to remain calm and talk to her in a calm and mature fashion. I told her that she was going to go manic without her medicine and that she could not stay there. Charles could not stay with her because he was vulnerable and she could be dangerous. She had already attacked Charles with a bowl of fruit that she tried to hit him on the head with. She said she just wanted to do things her way; she hated taking the Lithium that she was on at the time. She said it made her feel like she had the flu all the time and she just wanted to see for herself what would happen. I said OK and called the doctor that she had dismissed, because I needed help now with what to do. He was very patient and told me to make sure my dad did not return home. He said to take the car away from her because if she was manic and got into the car she could hurt someone else. My dad, as her spouse, would be liable for her actions. He said for us to stay away from her, but to make sure she had everything she needed as far as food and comforts. We were instructed to just watch from a distance, and be there when she crashed. Then he said that I could not call him any more because she had dismissed him and by law, he was not able to help us anymore. His last words were good luck.

So now Tim and I had a hypo-manic mother at home by herself. She was in non-compliance with her prescribed medicine and was also now not under the medical care of a professional. Tim and I went to our parents' small town and told the police the situation. We then went to all the neighbors and told them that she was at home alone and not taking her medicine.

Chapter 8

Fortunately one of the neighbors was the owner of the local grocery store. We asked him to bring home whatever food and items she so desired. We told Dorothy to just call him for anything she needed, which she did. I took Charles home with me to Texas where we waited for the inevitable, the "monster" to raise its ugly head again.

The whole town knew she was home alone, especially the church people and the police. They also knew she was not taking any prescribed medicine for her disorder. I am sure they did not really believe what we were saying. We had always protected Dorothy from anyone really knowing just how insane she could be. We would just usher her off to the hospital at every episode of mania she had.

In the meantime, from Texas I called every psychiatrist in Shreveport to try to get one to take Dorothy as a patient when she went manic. The family still did not want her to be in the charity hospital, which is where she would go if she did not have a private doctor.

Finally, one doctor in the whole city would even agree to talk to Tim and I about our mother. We went in to this new doctor's office for a consult. His name was Dr. Scott. He sat Tim and me down in his office on his couch. He did not appear to be very friendly. We told him this bizarre story of the life of our mother, Dorothy. We explained how she was now in non-compliance with her prescribed medicine and we knew that soon she would be out of control and home alone. We also explained that she had dismissed her last doctor because she thought he was trying to kill her. We desperately needed professional help for her safety and hopefully for her recovery.

He looked at us and asked, "What is it that you want for your mother?" We said we want our sweet mother back that we know and love when she is on her medicine. He smiled and said that was the right answer. He then agreed to help us. What a relief!!!! He said that he did not trust a lot of family who came in with stories like ours. Many people just want to put their loved ones away in an asylum for life. We did not want that, we just wanted her to take her prescribed medicine and get back to her normal state. Dr. Scott told us that when Dorothy gets manic and starts to do crazy things, the neighbors won't tolerate it, and they will call the police.

He said when they call you to tell you that the police are taking Dorothy to the hospital and ask which hospital do you want her taken to, take her to the private hospital. I will meet her at the ER and begin taking over as her doctor. We thanked him and left feeling somewhat relieved. I went back to Texas with Charles and we just waited. Dorothy then started to get worse everyday. She answered the phone and talked to us and we could tell that she was being very confrontational and agitated. She really hated Charles and threw everything in the house that belonged to him outside in the back yard. All of his clothes, personal items, music albums, pictures, and anything that reminded her of him were on the grass in the backyard. My parents had a freezer full of meat and vegetables. She cleaned the whole freezer out and put it into a garbage can in the back yard where it rotted in the hot summer sun. One of the neighbors saw all of this and called us to tell us. He then went over to their house and cleaned it up.

Dorothy spent a lot of her time now at the neighbors' houses. She would walk over and invite herself into their houses almost daily. She told them that her family was abusing her and the only thing wrong with her was the fact that her family was torturing and mis-treating her. According to Dorothy, everything wrong with her was strictly the fault of Charles, Liz, and Tim. Of course the opposite was true and we were helpless in Texas. We did remain in phone contact with the neighbors and Dorothy.

Dorothy would get rides to the store and church with the neighbors. She always went to church because she believed that she was a direct messenger from God and tried to have a close relationship with the preacher.

She started ordering strange things from the store like cases of Ensure. She told me on the phone she was shrinking an inch every day and was very alarmed about it. She drank cases of Ensure everyday because she thought this would help with her shrinking problem.

She ordered cases of vitamins and gallons of milk from the grocery store neighbor. She requested delivery to her every day. He got very concerned about these orders and called Charles and I in Texas to ask whether he should deliver these things. We told him to take her whatever she wanted, because we wanted her to be comfortable. As she slowly started to become more delusional she called every distant relative that she could find the number for in her address book. She told them that she was being abused and needed them to come to her rescue and help her. These relatives were people she had not seen or talked to in years.

Dorothy also called Brigham-Young University in Utah, because her maiden name was Brigham and she tried to convince them that she was part owner of the university. She insisted they needed to send money to her so that she could fly up there for medical treatment. Indeed her maiden name was Brigham, but she had no relation to the university. She called my house in Texas about ten times a day, just to talk delusional nonsense. Most of the time she just wanted to scream vulgarities at me on the phone and insist I was a bitch and hang up. I had to start screening my calls because my sons were at home and were still quite young. I didn't want them to answer the phone and hear their grandmother telling them about God coming and how exciting it would be. She was creating a huge long distance bill that alarmed Charles. I called the telephone company and had her long distance services cut off. We still wanted her to have a telephone because we needed to be able to talk to her daily. We had to measure her degree of being manic or not. She imagined that her house was on fire and that I, Liz, am pregnant and trapped inside the house. She called the police and fire department and told them the house was on fire with me in it.

All the police and fire trucks arrived at the house where they found Dorothy hysterical and still convinced the house was on fire, but in reality it was not. They left and called Charles and I to tell us that Dorothy was getting very delusional.

We told them again that we appreciated the call but until she actually harmed herself or someone else, we were under medical advice to watch from a distance.

The police put her on their daily morning routine by patrolling by the house. They would check on her in her non-compliance delusional state of mind. Dorothy noticed that the police were coming by her house daily and she started to cook breakfast for them each day. They seemed to be having a grand time together having breakfast and coffee in her kitchen. We were actually comforted that someone was seeing her daily and watching her for us. Then one night the neighbors were awakened by Dorothy walking down the street at 200AM. She was naked and she started to beat on their windows with a stick. She was convinced their house was on fire and she wanted to wake them up to exit the house.

By now everyone in town were calling Charles and I, still waiting in Texas. They were very alarmed with her behavior and wanted us to know about it. We told them that our hands were tied because she had chosen to not take her prescribed medicine. Until she harmed herself or someone else, we could not do anything about the situation. No one could believe that we would not come to help her. Ralph was then home from New Guinea and went by to visit her. She had told me that Ralph was visiting her and I was glad.

Even if we had no contact with him I was glad that at least he was visiting his mother, as long as his wife did not go. He called me at my house to say that he had just visited Dorothy. He was concerned because she was very delusional.

I said thanks for telling me this and you can thank you wife for helping to create this situation we were in.

He said he was going to call the police to go pick her up the take her to the charity hospital. I told him not to do that because of several reasons. One, I felt she was not as bad as she would be later, and two, I did not want her to be taken to the charity hospital. But because his wife told him to call, he did. The police arrived and dragged her screaming and kicking out of the house. They physically restrained and took her to the charity hospital where for the first time in her life she was not in private care. I am sure the charity hospital has an excellent psychiatric-ward, but this was never what we wanted for her. Charles, Tim, and I were very upset. This new situation started another round of anger and crying.

After seventy two hours they called me from the charity hospital and instructed me to come pick her up. This was no surprise to me. A mental patient when taken into these psychiatric wards is given a cognitive test of thirty questions and can only be held for seventy two hours for observation.

Dorothy had taken that test so many times before; in her semi-delusional state she passed it perfectly and held herself together for the required seventy two hours.

This was enough to be sent right back home. I drove over from Texas and walked into the charity hospital psychiatric-ward, checked her out. I took her back home, just like I knew would happen.

After that she got very bad mentally. The last straw was when she started to just walk into the neighbor's houses without even knocking. She just walked in with a pair of scissors in her hand and tried to climb up on their kitchen table where they were sitting having their morning coffee.

She said the government was spying on them and she had to cut all their electric wires around the light fixtures because there were listening "bugs" placed in them. I am sure she had not slept in a week and she had her usual manic look of dark circles under her eyes, hair not combed for days and that wild eyed look. Just as Dr. Scott had told us, the neighbors, normal people, could not tolerate this anymore and once again the police were called to come get her. This time they called Charles and I and asked where to take her and I directed them to the private hospital and I called Dr. Scott. The neighbors said when the police arrived and saw how sick she was, they asked "Where is this woman's family?"

We were there, only from a distance, doing what the medical professionals told us to do. We were to keep our blind father from her and watch and take care of her needs until she crashed. I told Dr. Scott she was on her way to the ER and was very delusional. The neighbors had called just like he had told me they would. He said thanks and that he would meet her there and take over as her physician. Since she was in non-compliance and being brought in by the police, my power of attorney would allow for us to admit her, even against her will.

I packed up Charles and we went back to Louisiana. I went to the hospital first and filled out all the paper work. I met with Dr. Scott at the hospital also. He said after his initial evaluation that everything I had told him about her manic-depressive state was correct. She was so bad that he had her in a double lock down padded area on the 8th floor of the hospital psychiatric-ward. The family was very saddened by how sick she was but relieved that now she couldn't hurt herself or scare the neighbors.

When I went to her house I found lots of interesting things. She had taken all the door knobs off every door of the house inside and outside. She had cut down every ceiling light fixture from every room in the house and placed them on the dining room table. She was convinced the government was spying on her and she was trying to stop that.

I went to the hardware store and bought all new door knobs. She not only had removed them all, they were no where to be found. I called an electrician to come put the light fixtures back in their proper places. I finally had to do a major cleaning of the house. The neighbors then all came over and were incredulous about how sick she was. They had never seen someone delusional before. They were apologizing to us for believing Dorothy when she told them we were abusing her. I told them that we had been living with this situation, this "monster" for forty five years and that they should have believed what we were saying was true. All those years we had protected Dorothy because we did not want anyone to see her like that. Now it was all out in the open for all to see.

Chapter 9

The first hospital stay under the care of Dr. Scott was probably one of the most exciting Dorothy ever had. Try as he might, this new doctor still could not get her to take any anti-psychotic drugs. Dorothy continued in her manic frame of mind. Of course, God was coming again. Wasn't He just here a few years ago? (How many times does He have to make an appearance?) This time Dorothy did not want to hear what he was saying. Ironically, God was talking to her from inside the toilet in her room. So she, ever so cleverly, placed the only straight back metal chair in her room up against the closed door knob. She then stuffed all her towels into the toilet, so she could not hear God talking to her. She then began flushing the toilet, with the towels stuffed in it until she flooded the entire hallway of the hospital's psychiatric ward before the nurses and aides could get her door open. After this manic episode she enjoyed her stay there with the door removed from the hinges so she could easily be observed by the staff.

Another time while I was talking to her on the phone, she was convinced that there were ants everywhere. They were on the floor, in her bed, and covering the phone. These ants had her so angry, that she started beating the phone with the phone receiver and smashed it to bits. After that she had no telephone in her room.

Dorothy was still convinced that the government was still spying on her. She thought they were poisoning her food. Once while I was visiting her, she took her lunch tray and started yelling at the nurse who was sitting at the control desk in the middle of the psychiatric-ward. She was telling her that her food was poisoned. She threw that tray across the desk at the nurse where it landed in her lap. The nurse then escorted me out and dealt with Dorothy in her own professional manner. Dorothy was also convinced that the coffee pot at that nurse's station was poisoned. Every time the nurses made coffee, Dorothy would sneak in and dump the fresh pot of coffee down the sink. She did this so many times; the nurses told me they had to stop making coffee because they were afraid Dorothy would burn herself.

Every time she went into the hospital we had to put her name on all articles of clothing with a permanent marker, like going away to camp. We had packed for her all the essential items of clothing like we always did. After one day the nurses called me to say that she did not have any clothes and that I should bring her some more. At first I was fine with this, so I packed her a second set of clothing and took it, with her name on it to the hospital.

The next day I got another call to say that her clothes were missing again. I asked the nurses what was going on. I did not have the money to continue replacing her clothes every day, especially considering that she usually stayed for three months.

We needed to solve this problem. Were they stolen, lost in laundry, or what? I took a third set of clothes to the hospital in hopes that the staff could figure out the problem. The next day they called to say that Dorothy had been observed giving her clothes to the other patients. She was also throwing them into the trash, or flushing them into the toilet. I decided that until she took her medicine and stopped being in a manic state of mind that she was just going to have to wear a hospital gown. I could not keep playing this game with her. This made Dorothy very angry at me for not helping her.

Dorothy started to call everyone in our small-town to tell them how I was abusing her. She had to walk around naked, or with just a hospital gown on. When she originally packed for this hospital stay, she packed her address book. She had every relative and friend's phone number at her disposal. She continually called and told them all about her being abused by her family.

The psychiatric-ward, by law, has to keep available a public telephone. Typically it is located in the hallway. That was the one she was using because she had smashed her phone because of the ants.

Therefore, all the people of small-town, USA started calling me to say that Dorothy was calling them with wild ideas about the government and family abuse. They wanted to know if I could do something about it. I told them that the law states that she must have full access to a telephone, even if she is in a double locked down psychiatric-ward. I could not do anything about it. This was our government tax dollars at work.

Dorothy, from that public phone called J.C. Penney's, the Department store, where she convinced the clerk on the phone to open a personnel charge account. She then charged $ 500.00 of clothing and asked the clerk to just bag it up. Someone would be there to pick it up for her. She then called a cousin of mine, who sometimes would befriend Dorothy. I never had contact with this cousin.

Dorothy told this cousin that she was in the hospital and that I had been abusing her and not allowing her to have any clothing. Dorothy requested that she pick up these clothes at Penney's and bring them to her in the hospital. My cousin, with good intentions, I am sure, actually did this and took Dorothy the clothing.

The next day, I got a call from the nurses explaining what had transpired and to tell me that Dorothy still did not have any clothes because those new ones were already gone. I never told my cousin about how Dorothy had been throwing away, flushing, or giving away all of her clothing; I knew she was just trying to help her aunt.

The next month Charles got the charge account bill of $ 500.00. He called a manager at J.C. Penney and explained that his wife had called from a public phone in a double locked down psychiatric-ward where she was severely mentally ill. She had convinced his clerk to open a charge account. Charles also explained that since she was in the hospital, that he was not going to pay this bill. She was in the hospital under a coroner's commitment, because the police had taken her to the hospital.

Charles said if you don't believe me just check the coroner's files, because it was public record. The next day this manager called Charles and said that the charges for the clothes would be dismissed. His company could not enter a contract with someone who had been committed under orders of the coroner. He apologized and said that Charles would not hear anything about this again.

Several other things were brought to Charles's attention after Dorothy would make calls from that public phone. She called a housing contractor and had him ready to come to their house and build a new fireplace with an open pit. She also tried to re-buy some land that Charles had recently sold to pay her hospital bills. She was trying to buy it back, because, of course, God was coming. She was one of two prophets that were going to help him. Dorothy needed that land for the coming of God.

Then it was another Mothers day and she was still in the hospital. This was so very sad for Tim and me. We came from Texas and took her a beautiful Easter Lily plant and tried to visit her as well as one can visit someone who is manic. Before we could even get home the nurses called to tell us about that plant we had just given our mother. She had wadded it up into a small ball and was bowling with it up and down the hallway of the psychiatric-ward. So much for feeling sorry for her as it was very hard to suppress out disappointment and anger. We certainly should have known better, but it was Mother's Day. As usual with all major holidays when Dorothy was in the hospital, the family always visited her.

Chapter 10

All of this time Dorothy's new doctor, Dr. Scott, was slowly trying to gain her trust and convince her to take her medicine. She still steadfastly refused to take it. Psychotic people are really very mentally ill, but they don't realize it. They are so convinced that their way of thinking is correct and can't be swayed to believe anything else. Dr. Scott called a family meeting and said he didn't think he would succeed with her. He recommended that we take Dorothy to court to have her involuntarily committed.

This was the second set of psychiatric medical staff to tell us this. It was still something we did not believe we could live through. Dr. Scott gave us a list of attorneys who specialized in this type of litigation. He told us to call one, because he could not leave Dorothy in the hospital forever. Soon she would have to be discharged, manic or not. Hearing this, we immediately called an attorney and scheduled a meeting with him.

Charles, Tim, and I started the proceedings of suing our mother for being in non-compliance with her medicine. This was a very un-real experience. I have learned to not say that I will never do something, because I had said I would never take her to court. Here we were, doing just what we swore we would never do to her. It was obviously for her well being. We did not want her on the street in a manic state of mind.

The state, upon hearing someone in a mental ward is being sued to be committed against their will, appoints a patient advocate attorney for that patient. Dorothy got a weasel looking man who does a good job of representing her in court. The family knew he did not have the same interest in our mother's safety as we had.

Charles, Tim, and I arrive at the courthouse in downtown Shreveport and entered a room with Dr. Scott and Dorothy. Dorothy was accompanied by her attendant who had brought her from the double lock down psychiatric area. Also present were her weasel advocate and the judge. After hearing professional opinion from Dr. Scott that Dorothy was in non-compliance with her prescribed medicine and was functioning in a manic state and after hearing from the weasel attorney, the judge ruled that Dorothy was not going to be committed against her will. She had to be discharged from the hospital in two days by court order. We were shocked and were again at a loss for words.

Two days later, Tim and I, and our estranged brother Ralph, arrive at the hospital to take Dorothy home. We left Charles at home because we knew that in her delusional state, she was still blaming him for all her problems.

In the day room where all the psychotic patients gather, we found Dorothy sitting in a chair. She knew we were coming to take her home and that she was under a court order to be dismissed from the hospital. She refused to leave with us.

She sat in the chair and said that she was comfortable in the hospital and that she was not leaving. No matter what we said or the nurses said, Dorothy would not get out of the chair and leave with us. The doctor and hospital administrator were called to come and they both told her that she had been discharged and must leave the hospital. She still would not get out of that chair and leave. So the doctor called the judge on the phone and told him what was going on. She was delusional and would not leave the hospital even under court order.

The judge said, "You have twenty four hours with her in the hospital, then, even if you have to get security to physically carry her to the sidewalk, she must leave the hospital". The doctor turned to us and said, "Your mother is twenty four hours from being a street person, if I can't get her to take her medicine". Another day in the life of dealing with bipolar disorder as an unrelenting monster.

Tim and I went to Charles's house where he was staying with his companion, and care giver Mary. When we told him the most recent story of how she would not leave with us, he fainted and collapsed on the floor. We were all worried that he was having a heart attack and rushed him the emergency room. Tim and I again looked at each other. There we were in two different hospitals, in one day with each of our parents.

I felt like we were on a carnival ride that we had no control over. All we could do was just hang on and try to survive it. Thankfully, Charles had an anxiety attack, not a heart attack. The mental pressure from worry about his wife was taking a real toll on all of us, especially him.

That night Dr. Scott called me and asked, "In the past, did your mother receive shock treatments?" I said yes, but they were so archaic and barbaric that we promised her that she would never have them again. We would never sign for her to have them. "But, "he asked, "Did they work when she did have them?" I told him that to my knowledge they did. He said he was going to, as a last resort; try to get her to take one small shock treatment. He explained that shock treatments were much better now. The patients were medicated before the treatment, and therefore she would feel no pain nor have any distress. I told him I did not think she would consent. One time when she was on the phone with me while standing in the hall of the psychiatric-ward, some orderlies came up the hall pushing a gurney. She started screaming bloody murder into the phone. She thought, and was afraid; they were coming for her to take her for shock treatments.

I finally got her calmed down and convinced her that the orderlies were not coming for her. Dr. Scott said he had instructed his staff to go home and pray for Dorothy. He was going to as well, and see if the next morning she would consent.

He said he would call me. I had never had a doctor get down to the last resort of praying for a patient after all other things had been tried to no avail. I knew then that this doctor was special.

The next morning, Dr. Scott called me to say that Dorothy had signed the consent and they were medicating her. Soon they would be taking her for the shock treatment. I could not believe it. You never know from day to day what a bipolar person will or won't do.

No predicting, as it is always a very frustrating guessing game. Later that day I was sitting on the floor of my bedroom folding clothes that I had taken from the dryer. The phone rang and my mother in a very shaky and quivering voice said, "They tell me I have been very sick".

I dropped the phone and started sobbing into my hands. It was immediately obvious to me that my wonderful mother was back in the real world after one small shock treatment. A shock treatment I never thought she would consent to. The monster had lost this battle thanks to Dr. Scott and the power of prayer.

She was not going to be a street person after all.

After that day she started to trust and actually love Dr. Scott. He convinced her to finally take a new anti-psychotic drug that worked for her quite well. I set her up in an assisted living facility where she could have excellent care around the clock. She had food and activities, and most importantly, someone to help her with her daily drugs.   When I took her there from the hospital, I had a frank conversation with her. We talked about how she could not live in the "real "world without medicine. We would find the best medicine available that she liked. She agreed and all was well for a while. She fit right in at this assisted living and started to make new friends. The staff got used to helping her with her medicine every day.

After about one year, the medicine once again, stopped working and we entered the same process of God coming again. Dorothy was becoming more and more delusional. One day early in the morning,

Dorothy arrived at the breakfast table with all of the old retired people. She was naked and had two sharp knives in each hand. The "monster" had reared it's ugly head again.

One of the staff called me and asked what to do, I said take her to the hospital. I called her doctor to meet her there. They did this after convincing Dorothy to get dressed. They then told me that they could not keep someone "like her" at their fine establishment. I was asked if I would come and get her belongings out of her room.

When I went to the assisted living facility, the staff told me they had never seen anyone act like that before. They were so shocked. I thanked them for their help and went looking for a new facility who would take someone "like her" when she got out of the psychiatric-ward this time.

Dorothy did really well in the hospital this time and did not stay too long before Dr. Scott dismissed her. We went once again to get her from the hospital and take her to a different assisted living facility. This new facility said they could handle a bipolar patient as long as she took her medicine.

Chapter 11

I really liked this new assisted living facility. The ladies there were very friendly and stayed busy with arts and crafts. Dorothy was starting to act kind of reclusive and she knew she did not fit in. No matter how many times the ladies graciously invited her to join them, she refused. Everything went well until Dorothy had what the doctors thought was a stroke. The staff found her on the floor of her room. She was un-responsive and they rushed her to the hospital ER.

The doctor there was an old friend of mine from high school. He said that the CT scan and MRI results of Dorothy's brain showed no evidence of a stroke. However, there was a lot of early atrophy. He thought it was a stroke but was puzzled because it should show more definitely on the medical tests.

I remember staying with her one night in the ICU and she looked terrible. She was basically not responding and one side was slightly paralyzed. The hospital staff talked to me about her living will and I had to make sure they had a copy on file. This scared me. I was afraid she was dying already.

I stood by her bed side and fed her ice chips with a spoon. She always loved to eat ice. She would open her mouth, with her eyes closed and eat the ice. I talked to her and I knew she knew I was there with her. She came out of this very fast and went back to the assisted living.

Her ability to walk was starting to be impaired and she was continuously passing out and being taken to the ER. It seemed like this happened every week. The doctor could not see any evidence of a stroke. On one visit I asked this friend of mine to release her medical records to Dr. Scott. I wanted her psychiatrist to see what he knew about what was happening with her. After reviewing the records, Dr. Scott called to say that he knew what was going on. After taking anti-psychotic drugs for forty five years, they had started to kill off the brain cells. He said this was what was happening with Dorothy. In his experience, the part of the brain that controls your ability to walk is usually affected first.

Dorothy's brain cells were now dying and she started to use a walker to walk up and down the hall at her assisted living facility. She started to not be able to eat by herself and her walking continued to get worse. The staff told me that the only way they could keep her was to place her into their Alzheimer's unit where the residents are locked in and stay together. We moved Dorothy into that area where she had some good and some bad days.

Once I went to get her to take her out to dinner and shopping. When I arrived the nurse told me Dorothy had a bad night. I asked what you mean. Dorothy had been standing inside her bedroom door and knocking. She then would open the door to see who was out side the door. All the time she was the one knocking from the inside.

She had done this all night long.

Some other stories about her failing mental condition involved her lapses in memory. One time she turned on the shower to get warm before getting in, then sat down in her chair and forgot the shower was running. She flooded her whole bedroom that time. Another time the staff let her walk around the whole assisted living for some exercise. She got tired and just lay down on the floor in an upstairs hallway and went to sleep right there. That was when this fine establishment asked us to move her to a complete nursing home because they could not give her the attention she required.

Once again, we packed up her things and had to set her up in a nursing home. She then started to use a wheel chair as her brain cells were continuing to die and she could not walk or stand without help. This place did the best they could, but Charles, Tim, and I did not like it. They put her into a room that was very small with another lady and Dorothy did not like this.

They did not have a different room so we moved her once again to a different nursing home; into a private room.

Her health deteriorated until she had to have someone feed her all her food. Her right side was paralyzed, leg and arm. I asked Dr. Scott if she had to continue taking all her anti-psychotic drugs since they were killing her brain cells. He said her chemical balance was so fragile that he was afraid to try to change anything.

One weekend the staff at this nursing home called me to say she was having grand-mal seizures and they took her to the hospital. The MRI scan of her brain just told the same story, her cells were dying and she had severe atrophy. Other complications arrived as Dorothy's mental atrophy worsened.

While she had been using the bathroom and one of the attendants was helping her to turn and get back into her wheel chair, her ankle broke by the twisting action. Dorothy was sent to have her leg put into a cast. Dr. Scott called to tell me that she had only about six months to live and to call in hospice if we wanted to. How ironic that the anti-psychotic drugs she required to live in the normal world were the very drugs that would ultimately kill her. I am convinced that if she did not take these lethal prescribed anti-psychotic drugs. she would have been eventually committed against her will to an asylum, or would have ended up as a street person.

What sad and very realistic choices these bipolar people have, brain killing drugs, asylums, or living on the street. Six weeks later, on the day of her death, she was still taking 1250 milligrams of an anti-psychotic drug for this "disorder bipolar".

Chapter 12

And then after all that there is an image you have. The image of your blind father inside the ICU, brailing his wife – feeling gingerly every tube in her body and asking what each one is. I did not have the courage to do this with him because I had seen him do this previously when the doctors thought she had a stroke and she was in a quasi-coma. Tim, ever so wonderfully went into the ICU with him. I had already seen her in the ICU. I could tell her spirit had gone to another place, there was no warmth, and her body's skin was mottled, and her limbs were cold. I knew she was free finally of that chemical imbalance that had plagued her for life. Ironically, Tim and I were at the funeral home taking care of her last funeral arrangements and the director, just being nice, asked us what our mother had died from. We told her that Dorothy had been bipolar and the anti-psychotic drugs had slowly taken a toll on her brain and caused brain death ultimately. The director, who was there to help and console us, got tears in her eyes and explained that her son had just been diagnosed as being bipolar. She was very afraid and upset.

I looked at her with the utmost sympathy and asked her not to judge us where we were now at the end of a life journey with our bipolar mother. I never felt sorrier for anyone in my life. I knew the many years she had ahead of her dealing with her son's "monster".

Dorothy looked so beautiful in her casket dressed in "hot pink", one of her favorite colors. I could tell she had a peace that she had never known. The daily regiment of brain killing anti-psychotic drugs, the forty eight years of being excited about the return of God, and the everyday battle with violent mood swings, all of these things had died along with her body. I knew her spirit had finally met the God she so badly wanted to meet while she was on earth.

We lost the woman who gave us life, but we gained a tremendous sense of freedom and peace ourselves. Freedom from a disorder that had been a dark cloud over our heads for forty eight years. I felt a shocking sense of sadness, but more of relief. Relief that the long ordeal was finally finished and that I could sleep un-afraid at night and actually maybe, leave the closet door open.

Ralph and I told Charles that even through all the ordeals with Dorothy that we were glad he had kept our mother in our lives and did not commit her to an asylum in her early years. We assured him that we thought he had made the right decision no matter what. But Tim had a different point of view that I thought was interesting and sad.

He said he thought he would have been better off not knowing her while growing up. Tim has been a step-father to two wonderful children who are now adults. He has a great and fulfilling relationship with them. He feels that knowing what he knows about the love between a step parent and step children cause him to feel differently. He wished he had a step mother as a child who was normal and would have loved and nurtured him in a positive way. I initially thought this was sad, but I understand it and accept it. I respect it as his point of view that I don't have.

Don't ever ask, "Where is this woman's family?" to us!

We were there always and never left Dorothy,
We were the ones, who took care of Dorothy even when she called us a bitch and bastard,
We were the ones, who took Dorothy to the hospital when she was delusional,
We were the ones who walked out of the double lock down psychiatric ward crying as we heard Dorothy screaming for us to come get her out,
We were the ones, who pushed the down button on the elevator crying,
We were the ones, who protected Dorothy and cleaned up after her delusional nightmares,
We were the ones, who stayed with Dorothy when everyone else left,

We were all victims, with Dorothy.

Dorothy's wedding picture at 20 years of age.

Epilogue

This book, of course, is dedicated to Charles, Tim and Ralph. A special thanks to Charles for making the best decisions he could with a very mentally sick wife. Thanks also to Charles for allowing us to know who our mother was as well as we could know someone who is highly medicated and severely bipolar. I wish him every happiness now in his latter life. He earned every minute of it.

Another huge thank you to Dr. Scott, who helped in ways unexplainable, with Dorothy's second half of her life and through her death. He was recently killed in an automobile accident driving to take care of some of his patients. The psychiatric medical world lost one of its best.

To my husband, Gerard thanks for sleeping on the side of the bed closest to the closet door for the past twenty eight years and knowing that if we happened to go to bed with the door open, you knew without being asked that you had to get back up and close the door.

The last thank you goes to Mary, who is now Charles's wife. I thank you for being with us in Dorothy's second half of life. I thank you for helping with her in all the ways that only you know. I wish you the same happiness as Charles for the rest of your lives.

In retrospect, after having written this very personal story, maybe I did have some therapeutic gain. It is obvious, even to me that I had a lot of pent up anger about this "disorder/monster". This disorder robbed us of knowing our real mother. I am sure that the anger was an underlying emotion that encouraged me to put this story into print. We never talked about bipolar much as a family. We were just trying to survive. I encourage everyone who is bipolar or who is the caregiver of someone who is bipolar to "embrace" it. Let it lie out like an open wound, so that later you don't remove the scab only to find that it is still bleeding.

This book is also dedicated to every "victim" of this disorder, this "monster", bipolar. All of the victims; the parents, the children, the loved ones, the spouses, the diagnosed patient, and the significant others, of anyone who is diagnosed as bipolar.

About the Author

I just wanted to share my experiences with other people who are caring for a bipolar loved one. Our mother died two years ago and I wanted her story to be told. It is very personal, but I want to use what I learned to help other family members. I want them to know that they are not alone in the decisions they make everyday to help their bipolar loved one. I also wanted to show that the mental illness medical world is doing the best job they can. This story shows that the "system" itself does not work here in America and our mentally ill loved ones need more help. I appreciate all who read this and hope that this story helps in any way.